# Being Me

Written by Julie Broski
Illustrated by Vincent Vigla

Children's Press®
A Division of Scholastic Inc.
New York • Toronto • London • Auckland • Sydney
Mexico City • New Delhi • Hong Kong
Danbury, Connecticut

**Rookie**
READY TO
**LEARN**

## Dear Parents/Educators,

Welcome to Rookie Ready to Learn. Each Rookie Reader in this series includes additional age-appropriate Let's Learn Together activity pages that help your young child to be better prepared when starting school. *Being Me* offers opportunities for you and your child to talk about the important social/emotional skill of personal preferences.

Here are early-learning skills you and your child will encounter in the *Being Me* Let's Learn Together pages:

• Counting
• Narrative skill: describing

We hope you enjoy sharing this delightful, enhanced reading experience with your early learner.

4871 3779   6/12

Library of Congress Cataloging-in-Publication Data

Broski, Julie, 1962-
  Being me / written by Julie Broski ; illustrated by Vincent Vigla.
    p. cm. -- (Rookie ready to learn)
  Summary: A young girl tells what it is like being her, describing the things she likes to do. Includes sugges
learning activities.

  ISBN 978-0-531-26428-7 – ISBN 978-0531-26653-3  (pbk.)
  [1. Self-perception--Fiction. 2. Self-esteem--Fiction.] I. Vigla, Vincent, 1970- ill. II. Title. III. Series.
  PZ7.B7995175Bei 2011
  [E]--dc22

                    2010049906

CHILDREN'S PRESS, and ROOKIE READY TO LEARN, and associated logos are trademarks and or registered trademarks of Scholastic Library Publishing. SCHOLASTIC and associated logos are trademarks or registered trademarks of Scholastic, Inc.

1 2 3 4 5 6 7 8 9 10 R 18 17 16 15 14 13 12 11

I like playing dress up.
It's fun being me.

I can add and subtract.
I'm learning lots being me!

I like painting.
That's part of being me.

I can do cartwheels.
Watch out, I'm being me!

9

I like playing with friends.
I'm happy being me.

11

I help with chores.
I'm busy being me!

13

I like watching clouds.
It's peaceful being me.

I love reading.
It's exciting being me.

17

I enjoy planting flowers.
That's part of being me.

I love chocolate chip cookies.
I get hungry being me!

21

I can't hear.
That's part of being me.

23

I talk with my hands.
It's amazing being me.

25

We are so much alike,
but we have differences, too.

I love you for being you.

I know you love me for just being

# Congratulations'

## You just finished reading *Being Me* and found out how much fun doing what you like can be!

**About the Author**

Julie Broski lives in Kansas City, Kansas, with her husband, John, and three daughters.

**About the Illustrator**

Vincent Vigla studied graphics at the E.S.A.G.-Penninghen School in Paris. While there, he dreamed of one day working with American and British publishers.